PROMPT ME
SCI-FI & FANTASY

Creative Writing Journal & Workbook

By
Robin Woods

Epic Books Publishing

A boutique publishing company
Visit us at: www.epicbookspublishing.com

Lead editor: Beth Braithwaite
Additional editing: Tamar Hela
Beta Reader: Tessa Larrabee

Copyright © 2018 Robin Woods
First Edition

Cover Design created on Canva by Robin Woods

All photos in the "Picture This" chapter were taken by Robin Woods
Photo Notes: 1) My daughter; 2) Monmouth, OR; 3) Elevator doors in Seattle, WA; 5) Oregon Dunes;
6) Jellyfish at the Monterey Bay Aquarium; 8-10) Taken in Mariposa, CA;
12) Water Buffalo; 14) Oregon Dunes; 15) Carmel Mission

Illustrations in the "Chart This" Chapter are public domain offerings made available by
The British Museum. All originally published between 1850-1880.

Fonts: Calibri and Distant Galaxy

Summary: A wide variety of writing prompts for maximum inspiration.

[Creative Writing, Diary, Non-Fiction, Reference, Writing Workbook, Fiction Writing,
Writing Journal, Writing Reference]

ISBN-13: 978-1-941077-13-9
ISBN-10: 1-941077-13-7

Table of Contents

Introduction

Think of writing like woodshop. You have to build one piece at a time and refine the project after the structure is intact. Writing is sometimes messy, so we may need a little help with just getting started. When you begin to form your ideas, don't worry about grammar and punctuation. Simply getting the words down and experimenting is the most important part in the beginning. In order to become a better writer, you need to do three things:

1. Write often.

2. Read often.

3. Revel in the mistakes and learn from them.

So, embrace the mess and find your voice. Because as Stephen King once said,

> **"The scariest moment is always just before you start."**

Think of these pages as your workshop. Experiment with structure, color, and style. You never know; you may start something that grows into a masterpiece.

How to Use This Book

There are a variety of different styles of prompts in this workbook to help you decide what works best for you. If one style or prompt doesn't work, move on. If it doesn't work for you today, it might tomorrow.

If the pronouns don't work for you, change the she to a he or even something gender neutral. Prompts are meant to be inspirations, not shackles.

Carry it around with you. Mess it up. Use different kinds of ink. Stick Post-Its all over it.

Getting started is what's important. As prolific writer Louis L'Amour once said,

> **"Start writing, no matter what. The water does not flow until the faucet is turned on."**

Now, go forth and write!

PICTURE PROMPTS

It has often been said that a picture is worth a thousand words—but that doesn't really help writers. However, a picture can inspire thousands of words.

Use the following photos to create unique stories.

Writing Challenge:

Use at least three of the five senses in each of your stories.

☐ Sight   ☐ Taste   ☐ Touch   ☐ Smell   ☐ Hearing

There are charts in the reference section in the back of this book.

Picture Prompt How To

We are visual beings, so let's use our graphic nature to find inspiration. Following this page, you will find fifteen photo prompts. Use each of them as a muse for a story. It can be super short or the beginnings of a novel. This is a sample of what to do. When I see this picture, it makes me think about ancient castles and secret potions. So here is my story:

My fingertips were so raw that the whisper of air in the passageway hurt. I didn't know how many more creepy tunnels I could handle searching. That old crone now had every cent I'd saved for months; the information had better be good, or there would be some not nice words exchanged—*really* not nice words.

A shuffling of feet around the corner sent my heart into a sprint. With trembling knees, I forced myself to walk at a leisurely pace. Running would only draw attention.

Twenty steps to the next turn... fifteen... ten... five...one. A hand clamped down so hard on my shoulder that a whimper escaped my lips.

"Girl, what are you doing here?" a guard grumbled at me.

Gulping down a breath, I stammered, "B-b-beg your pardon, sir. The mistress sent me to the cellars for some root vegetables, and I've gotten turned about."

He pushed a meaty hand through some even greasier hair. "Move on. This area's off limits. Duke's orders."

"Yes, sir. Might I bother you for the way to the root cellar?"

"Down and make a left. The way you were going's only dusty old things that'll get you into trouble. Now, move on."

I curtsied, ducking past him, and headed towards the cellars. I stopped just after the turn and listened. The moment I heard him go back the other way, I bounded towards the "dusty old things" because I certainly planned on getting into trouble. The vial was calling to me. I just wished it would be a little more specific. I pulled at another loose stone, and then another. My raw fingers smarting. The last known mermaid was hunted down twelve years ago, and the Duke had her tears. I would find that vial if I had to search every, single crevice. I would claim my birthright...and then he would pay.

1. Title: _____

2. Title: _____

3. Title: _____

4. Title: _____

5. Title: _____

6. Title: _____

7. Title: _____

8. Title: _____

9. Title: _____

10. Title: _____

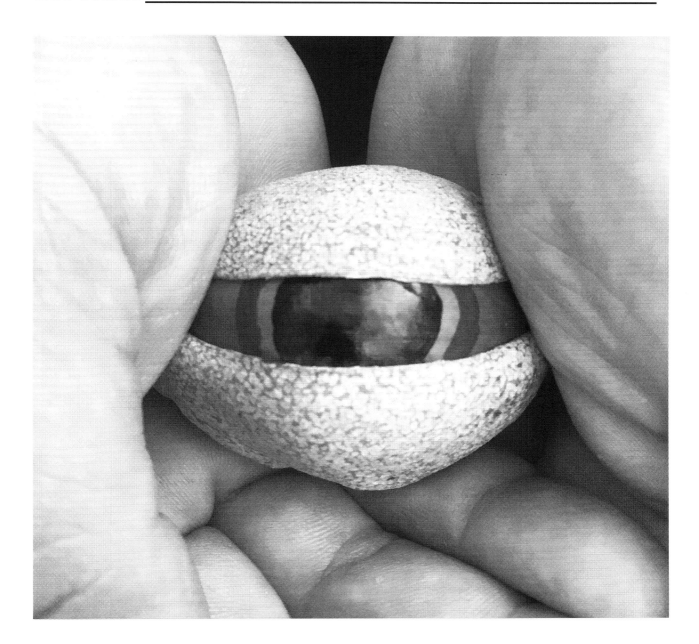

11. Title: _____

12. Title: _____

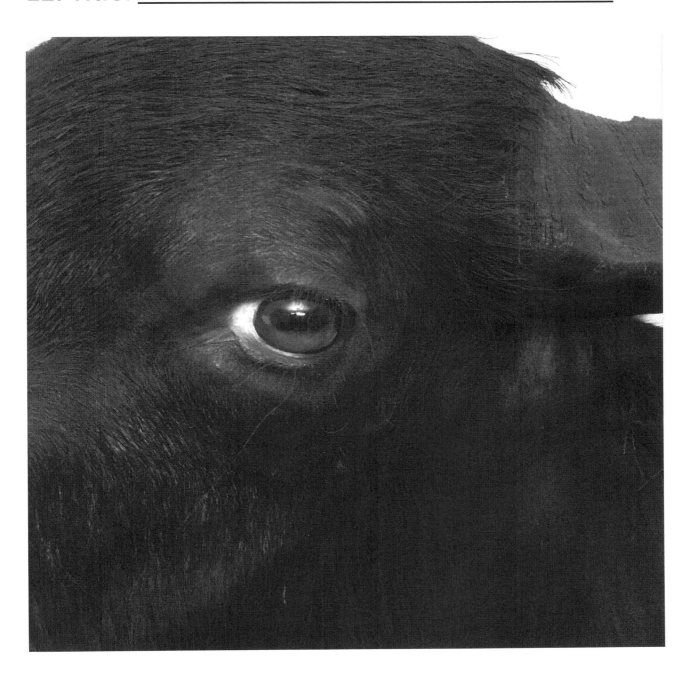

13. Title: _____

14. Title: _____

15. Title: _____

Prompt # _____ Your Title: _____

STORY STARTERS: FIRST PERSON

Emotional Standpoint: Subjective
View: Limited
Pronoun Usage: I/we/us/me/my/mine/our/ours

Writing Challenge:

Vary your sentence beginnings by limiting the number of sentences you start with "I" and "The."

FIRST PERSON

16. I watched as their souls flew from their bodies in a terrible roar...

17. The look in his eyes made me want to retreat into the depths of a cave and stay there forever, but I could see through his...

18. In the glow of the red moon, I could see what was normally hidden.

19. It was a well-known fact that the beasts of old were now extinct, but the evidence was saying that the elders' teachings were useless. Hot breath puffed on my neck from behind...

20. A thousand slithery things were alive down here with me...

21. Gentle sleep soothed me for the first time in weeks, yet I knew that when I opened my eyes, the scene before me...

22. I had about three minutes outside the airlock until my fingers would be too cold...

23. With my wands safely tucked inside the secret pocket, I shouldered my way into the bustling village, careful to avoid the eyes of the enforcers.

24. *Why would I use a sword when I have a perfectly good laser pistol? Oh...*

25. *"Heeeyyy*, monsters," I squeaked. "I am way too salty to eat...and I never take my vitamins, so there would be like, no nutrition." I eased out a shaky breath while...

26. Following procedure, I released the drones. But I knew it was a bad idea.

27. The distress beacon had been bleating for an hour before it roused me from a deep sleep. *Who had turned this thing on?*

28. For a second, his eyes glowed, but he quickly turned away. I had to know more, so...

29. An unfamiliar jingle weighed down his pocket. It took me a full three minutes to realize it was a bribe...and I was the one he'd given up.

30. Death didn't feel like I thought it would. This kinda tickled. But maybe...

31. He called himself a king. I would show him the wrath of a god. Power swirled in my belly with a quaking force that...

32. "Yeah, my kids say snuggling is my super power." I twirled my phaser stick. "*I think it's*..."

33. "Scavengers," I breathed. They'd taken over the whole west quadrant, and now they had reached the outer spiral. I had one chance at this...

34. The orb made no noise, but the terribleness of it seemed to bellow. Gritting my teeth...

35. There were only three keys left. Once they were in my possession, I would force the Zubayre to be happy. Like it or not.

36. *How stupid of them to be using phasers here. One wrong move and BOOM*. I aimed...

37. Three moons glared down at me, so I threw an arm over my eyes to block their accusations. I'd had enough of...

38. It wasn't just the trees that had eyes in this area. The very air seemed to be watching me...

39. I toed the edge of the water and nudged my companion. "He realizes that suit won't protect him, right?"

40. They were emitting heat, so I slid them into my inner pocket to keep me warm, but...

41. The behemoth of a machine loomed over me. I wasn't sure if I was supposed to get inside or push. The thought of trusting my life to...

42. My number one fear was the radiation. I jabbed the needle into my arm without...

43. Something was moving beneath the surface; every monster movie I'd ever seen flashed in my head. My feet had carried me...

44. It was definitely a distress beacon, but not like any I'd ever heard. A chill crept...

45. The sensation was more of a tickle at first, but then I realized that something had encircled both of my legs and...

46. Adjusting the translator, I blended into the undulating crowd without notice.

47. The nebula had beckoned to thousands because of its beauty; it was a shame they hadn't known about the Zavir earlier—small, burrowing, and deadly. I released…

48. Joy swelled inside me as the garbage vessel barreled towards me…

49. The box was teaming with ancient treasure—stones and gems more beautiful than I could have imagined. Before I could pocket a single trinket…

50. I groaned. The junkers were headed up the main drive again. With efficiency, I stashed the…

51. He had an unusual smudge on his index finger. I let my mind drift for a moment, only to realize that there was but one way to get a mark like that. A knot wedged in my throat as…

52. It was the smallest casket I'd ever seen…

53. The blast of the alarm jolted me from my sleep. I rubbed at my chest, trying to decipher what type of an emergency it was this time.

54. My horse was close to giving out. *Poor thing*. We both needed water and rest—fast. So…

55. Trolls. *Great*. I cringed, readying myself for the smell. That was almost worse than their arrogance—almost.

56. I stretched my wings for the first time since my escape—and it was…

57. The cops in this sector were like hellhounds. I needed to get back home; at least the police there were honest. They would understand my predicament, only…

58. "Pretty sure if we get any closer to that eruption, we're going to end up like Icarus," I spat.

59. The time machine doors snapped open, making me jump. I prayed we were in the right place this time—my immune system couldn't take another hit.

60. Wind whirred through the buildings, unsettling my wig. As nonchalant as possible, I smoothed it and tried not to itch under the edge of the blasted thing. Then, a voice…

61. It's…errr…*his* skin flared in a lightshow like a cuttlefish the angrier he became. I just hoped he didn't have an ink sack or projectile tentacles under that poncho. One last…

Prompt # _____ Your Title: _____

Prompt # _____ Your Title: _____

Prompt # _____ Your Title: _____

Prompt # _____ Your Title: _____

Prompt # _____ Your Title: _____

STORY STARTERS: THIRD PERSON

Third Person Limited
Emotional Standpoint: Objective
View: Limited
Pronoun Usage: he/she/it/him/his/her/they/their

Third Person Omniscient
Emotional Standpoint: Objective
View: Unlimited
Pronoun Usage: he/she/it/him/his/her/they/their

Deep Third Person
Emotional Standpoint: Subjective
View: Limited
Pronoun Usage: he/she/it/him/his/her/they/their

Writing Challenge:

Vary your sentence beginnings by limiting the number of sentences you start with "He" or "She," or "It."

THIRD PERSON

62. He took the vial like a striking snake. "This will make her love me?" he asked aloud.

63. On this pass, the raven dipped close enough for them to realize—it wasn't really a raven. It was a minion reporting back to...

64. The whisper of electricity gave them away; it would be only seconds...

65. When he pulled the object from the forge, quiet settled over the entire room. This was no ordinary...

66. The entrance gaped like a shrieking mouth...

67. Vibrations started deep beneath the churning cauldron before anyone knew something was terribly amiss. It was when...

68. Error messages were more common than the machines working. This is why the mechanic...

69. *They were no better than vultures*, he thought. Sweat dripped from his brow as the scuffing of boots drew near his hiding place...

70. His eyes scanned the figure in the window. "She is the anti-Christ incarnate, isn't she?"

71. The luminescence of the creatures sliding beneath the surface of the water was entrancing. It made...

72. She curled herself around the Infinity Cup, wanting nothing more than power.

73. "Then let us dare to be brave enough to face rescue," he offered, wondering if anyone was listening...

74. Tunnels sprawled beneath the city like a malevolent virus twining with its' victims.

75. When he went to leave, iron bars sliced the space in half and mist poured into the shed. He wasn't investigating; he'd been led straight into a trap.

76. Repulsed, she shrank away, groaning, "Stupid mouth breather." Only seven more...

77. *There isn't much repair work*, he thought. But then, the shredding of metal grew louder. His fingers flew over his last chance for survival with renewed…

78. The baron had used his witch to put a curse on the water supply. All who…

79. An expletive slid from her lips—her crew had left her behind. She pulled the tie from her hair and plastered a smile on her face. She'd hitch a ride to the next planet.

80. Moon dust was being pedaled as a healing elixir.

81. "Serpentine!" she screeched, warning her partners to dodge the archers. They had been trained in evasion, but…

82. They'd hoped to return before dark, but as the sun set, they knew that they'd have to face…

83. Her smile faded as she took in the man approaching, though the word "man" was a kindness. He'd given up his humanity long ago…

84. Gems, as far as they could see, adorned every wall of the cave. Then, hot breath…

85. He turned crimson as the realization struck him like a fist…the sacred objects he'd given everything to find, no longer held any power.

86. She snapped her fingers, and the insects scattered instantly…

87. He wondered what it would be like to live a different life, for people not to write him off the second they laid eyes on him, but that's how it was in the outer rim. The tattoo stripped…

88. Tittering echoed through the long hall. She braced herself and dragged the bag behind her…

89. Dumah cut the line again. It was already a surging pit of anger, and this type of power play was only…

90. The warble in her vision was getting worse; she could see glimpses through the veil…

91. Music throbbed in his head and through the walls as he stumbled around the marketplace. *There had to be an apothecary in this village*, he thought…

92. This was one of those times—where the zipper getting caught could actually kill a person…

93. When the guard raised his hand to the child, she could no longer stand idly by...

94. He shoved the plate away choking, "Too much pepper," then gulped down a few desperate swallows to quell the fire. As he wiped his brow with the napkin, he slid the knife...

95. Someone had punched a hole in the manifold...

96. Deep water was worse than space. They buttoned up the external thrusters and switched out the filters.

97. She must have been the inspiration for Helen, for Venus, for every bewitching beauty...

98. His smile widened when his mother opened the door, but her scream of warning broke him. He knew the people that were after them; she was dead, and he would be soon.

99. *The luxurious velvet felt both good and foreign*, she thought. *How odd for a simulation*.

100. Panicked cries came over the COMMS, "Ambush! We are getting slaughtered. Fall back. Fall ba—" Then the COMMS crackled with static,...

101. Representatives from all seven kingdoms were here, but something felt off.

102. Love and admiration overwhelmed her. She embraced them for long moments that seemed to stretch out before her, but then she remembered...

103. She squeezed her eyes shut. *The cryo-sleep will seem like a night, not nine months*.

104. He dragged his fingers down the case with the gentleness of a lover before popping open the sturdy latches. A toothy grin split his lips. "A shock canon *is* the perfect gift."

105. Distrust was a wedge their group couldn't afford; they had a common mission that...

106. The skeletal remains of the Eiffel Tower poked up through the ruble as a terrible reminder of the final stand that...

107. Winning meant freedom. Losing meant a lifetime of submission. He knew there was no way to win—fairly.

Prompt # _____ Your Title: _____

Prompt # _____ Your Title: _____

Prompt # _____ Your Title: _____

Prompt # _____ Your Title: _____

Prompt # _____ Your Title: _____

USE THESE PHRASES

Writing Challenge:

Make choices that stretch you as a writer. Try writing from a different point of view, even if it makes you uncomfortable.

Write a story using visual language. Add as many of these phrases into your story as you can, to work your brain in a new way.

108. Choose and use at least six of these ten phrases in an original story:

burned like acid rain	mewling cats
tart taste making him pucker	clucked his tongue
adrenaline surged	a hissing rush
staggered woodenly	heat sizzled
sparkling wit	stuttered incoherently

109.Choose and use at least seven of these ten phrases:

grit grinding underfoot	heart was painfully sprinting
drowning in words	pride soaring
snick of a closing door	quiet as crunching ice
blissful solitude	loathsome stranger
concealed greatness	bubbling anxiety

110. Choose and use at least eight of these ten phrases:

earthy smell of horses	chill of stone
clank of metal	bite of cold
whir of power	mossy face
spiraling downwards	tarnished crown
sound vibrating the bones	skidding to a stop

111.Choose and use at least nine of these ten phrases:

refined with age	charred beyond recognition
smoothed by weather	assessed the damage coldly
myths of old	cacophony of discontent
tattered parchment	savory smell of fresh herbs
zigzagged to the top	brush of dusty feathers

112. Choose and use at least nine of these ten phrases:

bathed in starlight	glimpse of movement
vibration of engines	exquisite beauty
shocking, bitter taste	deafening roar
woeful unpreparedness	chortled with delight
Miniscule-looking seed	trudged down the passage

CHOOSE A PATH

Writing Challenge:

Use at least three of the five senses in each of your stories.

☐ Sight ☐ Sound ☐ Hearing ☐ Taste ☐ Touch

You can also add a sixth sense.

Use the beginning of the prompt and choose the path you would like to use for your new story.

113. He entered the airlock with...

- ☐ an extra space suit.
- ☐ a wicked looking blaster.
- ☐ top secret papers.
- ☐ schematics of the command floor.
- ☐ orders to float his best friend.

114. The horses whickered at the disturbance...

- ☐ dwarves had secreted into the camp without a single warrior noticing.
- ☐ the sky opened up and thrashed at the valley, as if it were angry.
- ☐ someone nearby was using the dark arts.
- ☐ the signal fires at castle had been ignited.
- ☐ a ferocious clashing of swords could be heard in the distance.

115. A figure stood in the darkened doorway...

☐ pointing a Coalition phaser at me—and it wasn't set on stun.

☐ for a long moment before collapsing like a rotted log in a windstorm.

☐ before being flanked by an Elven king and the Troll Keeper herself.

☐ just as the stones on the north wall began to quake.

☐ holding the remote to the time machine.

116. The desert landscape...

☐ was filled with fantastic creatures spun from dreams.

☐ beat her down with heat and threats of death.

☐ gave them hope. The promised land was close.

☐ was an illusion to drive away those interested in the area.

☐ teamed with marauders who preyed on any who dared to enter.

117. A metal man...

- ☐ towered above the crowd on a pedestal.
- ☐ creaked his way through the courtyard of the castle.
- ☐ in appearance only, hid the flesh and blood beneath.
- ☐ no more; he was a living, thinking, and breathing creation.
- ☐ inserted the last of the stolen pieces into his chest cavity.

118. The smell of toast...

     ☐ wafted through the actors' camp.

     ☐ permeated the mess hall, making the soldiers grumble with hunger.

     ☐ made her wonder if she was having a stroke.

     ☐ was the first sign that the wizards were active.

     ☐ hit her with a jolt as memories blinded her.

CHART IT

Fill out the chart and write the backstory.

Writing Challenge:

Use as few adverbs as possible. Consider "—ly" the enemy!

The Revelation of the Mysterious Journal

What? Controlling Idea	
When? The Time	
Where? The Place	
Which? The Specifics	
Who? The Players	
Whose? Possession	
Why? The Reason	
How? The Way	

119. Your character comes into possession of a tattered, leather journal that has been locked away for over a hundred years. The following fragments are inside the journal:

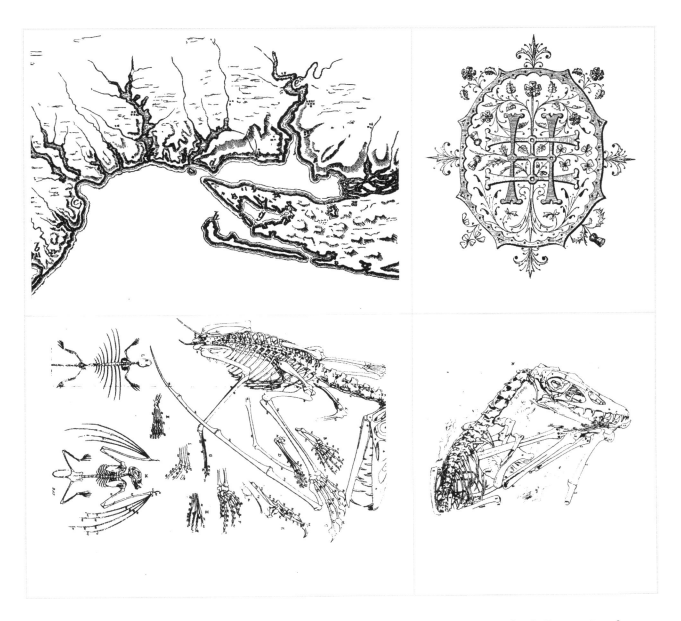

Answer the questions on the Mysterious Journal chart, and then use the information for your story.

The Treacherous Trunk

What? Controlling Idea	
When? The Time	
Where? The Place	
Which? The Specifics	
Who? The Players	
Whose? Possession	
Why? The Reason	
How? The Way	

120. Your character comes into possession of a trunk that was unearthed when a building constructed in the 1800s was demolished. The following items were inside:

Answer the questions in the Treacherous Trunk chart, and then use the information for your story.

Twisted Time	
What? Controlling Idea	
When? The Time	
Where? The Place	
Which? The Specifics	
Who? The Players	
Whose? Possession	
Why? The Reason	
How? The Way	

121. **Your character has been sent through time to save humanity, but has lost his or her memory. The only clues to the mission are the photos tucked into the inside pocket of his or her jacket. Now go, and save the world.**

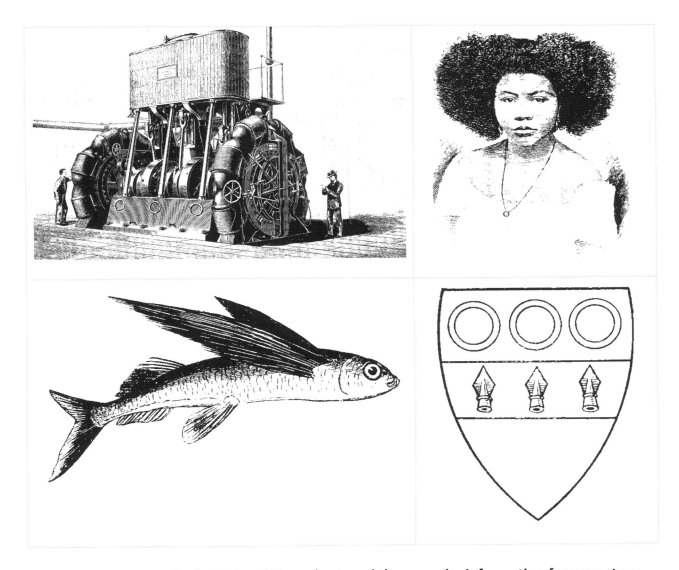

Answer the questions in the Twisted Time chart, and then use the information for your story. Additional notes:

122. Pick a main character from one of your stories and write their origin.

Main Character: ☐ Protagonist ☐ Antagonist

	Name	Meaning
First		
Last		
Middle		

PHYSICAL DESCRIPTION

Gender:	Age:	Birthday:
Height:	Weight:	Body Shape:
Eye Color:	Eye Shape:	Lip Shape:
Face Shape:	Nose Shape:	Ear Shape:
Skin Tone:	Skin Texture:	Nationality:
Hair Color:	Hair Texture:	Voice:
Facial Expression/Physical Ticks/Other:		

INTERNAL DECRIPTION

Personality Type:
Strengths/Talents/Powers/Skills:
Flaws/Weaknesses/Limitations:

Social Status:	Education:

Backstory: (Childhood, Romantic Relations, Philosophies, Etc.)

123. Pick a supporting character from one of your stories and write their origin.

☐ Sidekick ☐ Love Interest ☐ Mentor ☐ Fool ☐ Nemesis

	Name	Meaning
First		
Last		

PHYSICAL DESCRIPTION

Gender:	Age:	Height:
Eye Color:	Hair Color:	Weight & Body Shape:
Nationality:	Skin Tone:	Voice:
Facial Expression/Physical Ticks/Other:		

INTERNAL DECRIPTION

Personality Type:	
Strengths/Talents/Powers/Skills:	Flaws/Weaknesses/Limitations:
Backstory: (Why do we need this character?)	

DIALOGUE PROMPTS

Writing Challenge:

Use as few adverbs as possible.

☐ Play with dialect and the way your characters use contractions.
☐ Restarts, stumbles, and stutters can improve emotional scenes.

Dialogue Tips & Tricks

Each time a new character speaks, start a new paragraph.

A non-verbal physical response can be a "reply." So, it is often good to make that a new paragraph too. For example:

> Jane dashed into the room. "I've been looking for you everywhere."
> Fred shrugged, turning away from her.
> "You knew this was important to me." A small quiver in her voice betrayed her hurt.
> "Yup. I did," he said, flatly.

Pick a punctuation style and stick to it. Consistency is key. If you use an en-dash when a character is cut off in a conversation, do it *every time*. "No, but I jus—"

People rarely use each others' names in conversation after an initial greeting.

> "Heya, Eric."
> "Hello, Nora."
> "Eric, how has your summer been so far?"
> "Well, Nora, it has been rather busy. I'm ready to slow down for a bit."
> "I totally understand, Eric. I have been busy too."

> Besides the fact that the dialogue is a yawn fest, you can see that this feels very unnatural. It makes your characters sound like game show hosts. "Yes, Vanna."

Your characters should sound different. Your adults should not sound like teenagers, teenagers should not sound like collegiate scholars, and someone from Alabama should not sound like they are from Oxford, England. Play with dialect and the way your characters use contractions.

Read it out loud or act it out. This is the ultimate way to detect cheesy dialogue.

Generally, people speak in fragments. **What feels more natural?**

> *"Would you like to go and get some coffee with me?"*
> *"I would love to go and get some coffee, but I don't have any money."*
> *"I have money, so it's my treat."*
>
> **–OR–**
>
> *"Coffee?"*
> *He gave her a doe-eyed look. "You buying?"*
> *Chuckling, she rolled her eyes while grabbing her wallet. "Let's go, mooch."*

Silence can be powerful. When people speak to one another, there are often long pauses in the conversation. Let your characters and audience digest heavy information by giving them the break to process it. It will not only highlight the information, but give it emotional weight.

Here is a sample without the silence:

> *"I'm dying," he stated.*
> *She swallowed. "How long?"*
> *"Three months."*

The above conversation lacks emotional depth. Adding silence can increase the weight.

Here is a sample WITH silence:

> *"I'm dying." It was a simple statement—that changed everything.*
> *She sucked in a breath, but her eyes moved to the lake. The wind caressed the water, sending glittering ripples into the distance.*
> *After what seemed like forever, she swallowed. "How long?"*
> *Before answering, he let out the breath he had been holding in a slow stream. "Three months."*

Description should be given in small amounts. Unless your character is critiquing a piece of art, or analyzing something by pointing out details, don't have them say everything orally. I recently stopped reading a book because 95% of the character descriptions were in the dialogue. They were long, awkward, and felt like a list. Below, I have written a BAD example.

> He seductively pinned her to the wall, trailing his fingers across her jaw. She froze in fear as he leaned in even closer. His minty breath caused chills as he spoke. "My, what lovely eyes you have. They are such a unique color of blue—the specks of grey and whites almost make them look like the facets in a blue diamond. And your skin, it is so smooth I can't even see a pore on your face. It is the perfect balance of peaches 'n cream with a hint of olive. When I first saw you, I had expected your hair to feel different, but it is like fine, silken threads. It just makes me want to keep touching it. The color is mesmerizing, too. I can't decide if it is rich caramel or earthy amber. You are something, aren't you? You are the elixir I have been waiting for."

Really? Who would speak like that in real life? If they did, we would think that they were strange and try to avoid them.

Have fun writing your dialogue. The important thing is getting it on the page. Focus on 1-3 for now to help with clarity; the rest can be saved for edits.

124. "I would prefer it if you wouldn't die."

"No promises. That casket looks delightfully comfortable."

125. "If you need to kill a wolf, sometimes you need to sacrifice a few sheep."

"Ouch," she pouted, then feigned surprise. "Oh, you're implying I'm a sheep." She strolled around the room, allowing her heels to fill the room with a tick-tock sound. Then she continued, "That dry feeling in your throat? It isn't because you need water. I'll give you a hint: *I'm* the wolf."

126. "We are children of violence, and I intend to show you the condition of my mind." Electricity crackled between her fingers as the grin on her face unfurled into something unholy.

"Always so dramatic. You forget, darling, we have the same power."

She bowed her head for an instant. "True. At least...that was the case last week."

127. "Fabulous. Can't I have one day that isn't ruined by elves?"

"At least they smell good."

"In their human form."

128. "It is so nice when you leave."

"Awwww, I was just starting to get sentimental."

129. "The time of the Elders has past. It is time for new creation, new ideas, new—"

    "Aren't you an Elder?"

130. "Haven't you gotten the hint yet?"

"What hint?"

"Seriously? She chose prison over being with you."

FILL IN THE BLANK: 49 POSSIBILITIES

Writing Challenge:

Make choices that stretch you as a writer. Try writing from a different point of view.

131. I could smell the _____ **from that night and could feel**

_____.

Blank One	Blank Two
aromatic spices	the hammering of my heart
lingering fuel	his/her hands on me
vomit	the bite of the handcuffs
stale liquor	the joy of celebration
fruity bubblegum	the lightheartedness of childhood
birthday cake	the burn of hard work
bleach	the sheen of sweat on my forehead

132. **There were only three minutes left before the** _____, **filling me with**

_____.

Blank One	Blank Two
bomb blew	murderous rage
timer went off	bubbling excitement
class bell rang	unfathomable relief
launch	the need to destroy
surprise	paralyzing fear
shark feeding	the desire to go straight to bed
shift change	uneasiness

133. The water was _____ **as** _____.

Blank One	Blank Two
bubbling and warm	the animals gathered to drink
swirling in the cauldron	we eased into the hot tub
at low tide	I crawled across the desert
flowing steadily	the sun melted into the ocean
sparkling in my glass	we realized not all would survive
my only lifeline	we walked along the ragged shore
held back	the witches cast their spell

134. It spread _____, and everyone around _____.

Blank One	Blank Two
like a virus	moved towards the sweet aroma
its wings	avoided the sprouting vines
through the water	bounced with renewed energy
through the air	gagged and fell dead
joy	cautiously prepared to run
like it was sentient	bowed to the angel in fear
with wicked glee	understood what it meant

PERSON, PLACE, & THING

Writing Challenge:

Avoid the words "get" and "thing." Choose more specific language.

Person, Place, & Thing

135. Choose an item (or two or three) from each column, and use them to create a story.

Person		Place		Thing	
mechanic	countess	ship bridge	desert	ancient map	vial of liquid
scientist	toddler	garden	cave	ring of keys	stolen jewelry
alien	priest	castle	moon	waffles	bottle of soap
smuggler	musician	galley	underwater	piano	thorn bush
butler	cowboy	volcano	panic room	watermelon	list of names
farm boy	alchemist	throne room	rocky beach	deck of cards	pirate flag
translator	tracker	heath	tree house	stray dog	chewing gum
barbarian	ranger	boiler room	apartment	nuclear reactor	laser pistol
thief	tutor	pantheon	space RV	magical staff	armor
fighter	mastermind	carriage	bazaar	lunch meat	tin foil
ninja	grandpa	ice house	saloon	chocolate milk	hammock
healer	apothecary	island	asteroid	urn	lasso
pilot	berserker	swamp	weapons bay	statue	coconut oil
tinker	blacksmith	artist studio	museum	chainsaw	old parchment
banker	captain	shoe store	safe house	poison pill	lantern
mentalist	mariner	Ever Night	dragon lair	car battery	waterfall
time traveler	cartographer	wolf den	courtroom	zombie horde	dagger
philosopher	astronomer	train	gym	mirror	paperclips
Shadow Prince	sage	shack	ghost ship	ticking bomb	dagger
necromancer	butcher	underworld	Winterlands	diving suit	trunk
mutant	outlaw	outland	wastes	scorpion	flame thrower
innocent	tyrant	virtual world	outer planes	power crystals	toothbrush
misanthropic miser	mysterious stranger	Holy City of Lost souls	Forbidden Mountains	lightning generator	genie in a bottle
robot super servant	soldier of fortune	Forgotten Empire	Four Pillars of the Immortals	coupons for extra lives	safe that can't be opened
mystic defender	wilderness master	mad person's workshop	interstellar prison	quiver of arrows	cape of invisibility
Additional Ideas:					
Healing Pools of Elysium	Amulet of __	Gauntlet of __	Band of __		

You Name It

Compound names are the staple of fantasy stories. Winterfell, Who-ville, Neverland, Storybrooke, and Wonderland are all staples. Your mission is to create an outpost name.

136. Your character is headed to an outpost named _____ _____, when...

River	Thunder	Deep	Sand	Lair	Fortress
Oak	Wild	Reach	Cave	Sanctuary	Hold
Hill	Forgotten	Crest	Shire	Retreat	Encampment
Boulder	Forsaken	Storm	Pine	Camp	Den
Spear	Silver	Burn	Vale	Rampart	Refuge
Ever	Sorrow	Cross	Mist	Barracks	Frontier

_____

_____

_____

_____

_____

_____

_____

_____

_____

_____

_____

_____

137. Your Character has been falsely accused of a crime and has been callously tossed into a dungeon called The _____ of the _____ _____. What happens?

Broken	Thundering	Bones	Perishing	Vault	Cells
Lair	Violent	Unstable	Withering	Burrow	Maze
Burrow	Lost	Terrace	Dishonored	Tunnel	Pit
Haunt	Deadly	Sun	Fire	Quarters	Morass
Chambers	Crescent	Moon	Crypt	Point	Delves
Specter	Hollow	Mountain	Nightmare	Cavern	Tomb

138. Your character is a resident of the newest Space Station named _____ _____ in the Fulgora Galaxy. The station comes under attack and...

*(*Fulgora is the Roman god of lightning.)*

Blue	Prism	Prometheus	Nether	Sanctum	Terminal
Red	Revelation	Chronos	Sentry	Garrison	Colony
Silent	Neo	Zion	Dynasty	Keep	Base
Nova	Aura	Oracle	Wraith	Post	Haven
Mythic	Tranquility	Stealth	Solas	Bastion	Force
Union	Liberty	Republic	Fury	Sanctuary	Division

139. Your character wakes in a post-Apocalyptic land nestled into the broken passenger seat of The _____. A sound in the distance…

The Volcano	The Harvester	The Hydra	The Barrage
The Electric Guardian	The Warmonger	The Minotaur	The Blood Moon
The Trinity	The Rigor Mortis	The Wicker Man	The Super Nova

TRADITIONAL PROMPTS

Writing Challenge:

Avoid the words "get" and "thing." Choose more specific language.

Mixed Bag

Here's a little mix of different types of prompts to keep it interesting. Use these as a jumping off point to create your stories.

140. A mad scientist develops a shrink ray and wreaks havoc on the land.

141. After a solar flare, it is revealed when they can no longer make themselves invisible, that Gremlins really do exist in electronic equipment.

142. Pick five objects in the room. They are plotting to overthrow the known universe.

143. An empire rises from swamps located throughout the world. They command all reptile-kind and use them to subjugate humanity.

144. A meteor flashes through the sky. Afterwards, all animals can talk.

145. It turns out the "missing" thirteenth floor on all high-rise buildings is a command center for wizardry.

146. Top world leaders have been secretly bitten by werewolves.

147. Alarms across a city go off, and it is thought to be because of seismic activity. But days later, sinkholes begin to swallow up parts of town.

148. The International Space Station disappears and reappears five days later orbiting Saturn.

149. Children discover a memory eraser and use it on their parents to avoid getting in trouble. But they become addicted, and it soon spirals out of control.

150. Humans have genetic backups of themselves, but after a power surge, they all wake.

151. Citizens of the world are forced into military service at age sixteen. If you run, the government has to ability to turn back your clock to age twelve and train you in a camp.

152. A ship arrives on Earth with a list of requests for their dying planet.

153. A couple buys the home of a missing couple. When one of them leans against a built-in bookcase, a hidden door is revealed—and a new world.

154. Using magic starts to drain the world of resources. What resources and why?

155. The Tree of Life is found in a remote canyon in Africa. It still holds great power.

156. The new cancer immunization is embraced by everyone and it becomes mandatory, but within the next ten years, they realize all males have become sterile.

157. Famous literary villains from the past come to life after a legendary library burns down.

158. A crazy cult turns out not to be crazy. Aliens are caught abducting the citizens from an entire town. The cult had summoned them.

159. Once the polar ice caps melt to the appropriate level, Atlantis rises, ready for domination.

160. After a volcanic eruption, dragons wake and the power grid across the planet fails. Modern civilization has forgotten how to live without technology. It is a new Dark Age.

161. A classic fairy tale comes to life, but all the gender roles are reversed.

162. Guns become sentient and sense your intent before using them. If the shooter has ill intentions, the gun backfires.

163. Eye color changes with emotion, making it almost impossible to hide one's true feelings.

164. Dr. Jekyll's potion was real. It is tested on prisoners trying to rid them of their evil tendencies, but all doesn't go as promised by the drug company.

165. The Shadow World is revealed during a once-in-a-millennia solar eclipse.

166. The sky turned an eerie green again; the Fey had reopened the Gateway with their invasion forces.

167. Geneticists blend human and chameleon DNA and create half-breeds capable of invisibility.

168. An entire army vanishes, leaving nothing behind but armor and letters to their families. The only footprints are from the army entering the battleground—not a single one leaving.

169. All pets on the planet turn into balloon animals.

170. A woman wakes from a dead sleep when a voice in her room warns her, saying, "There is a predator outside." There is no one else in the room.

171. A man with special abilities can jump into any body he wants, but when he makes his latest hop, he enters at the exact moment another hopper takes the body. The host and the two hoppers all fight for control of the body.

172. Dinosaurs didn't go extinct—they went home. Now they're back.

173. Ogres start taking over freeway on and off-ramps. Major cities suffer gridlock and people abandon their vehicles in mass.

174. Zombies don't actually eat brains. They eat…

175. Shape shifters run the top tech companies in key cities throughout the world. It is all part of a master plan to…

176. Create a 1920s detective story in space. Have gangsters, flapper girls, and robots.

177. A couple is separated when their ship is attacked and their life pods go to separate planets. The communication unit is burned out in one pod.

178. An awkward first kiss leads to a building exploding. After that…

179. Humans are driven to living in trees, where they build elaborate tree houses. Why are they forced to do this?

180. Take your favorite Grimm's fairy tale and set it in either the modern world or the future.

181. Nano-bots are released in the water supply. People experience a rise in motivation and a feeling of euphoria, but then…

182. Vampires exist and can walk in sunlight.

183. People become addicted to virtual reality and lose track of their real lives in favor of the Realms.

184. The myth of a vain sprite who escapes a dragon's lair.

185. The journey of a goblin who has to decide whether to follow the path of his ancestors or blaze a new trail when his bravery is tested.

186. A tale of a mischievous nymph that can sink ships with a gesture.

187. Dragon bones are raised from the La Brea Tar Pits. The moment they are exposed to air, they…

188. A hermit holds the key to end a war. Finding him and convincing him to help will be epic.

189. Shocking crimes are happening at night. It turns out that the person responsible is sleepwalking. Weave a tale of intrigue.

190. A malevolent group uses cell phones to send subliminal messages while users are sleeping.

Prompt # _____ Your Title: _____

Prompt # _____ Your Title: _____

Prompt # _____ Your Title: _____

Make a List Of…

In Ray Bradbury's book *Zen and the Art of Writing,* he wrote that he made lists to help trigger ideas for writing. He states, "These lists … caused my better stuff to surface. I was feeling my way toward something honest, hidden under the trapdoor on the top of my skull." So, let's get to it and make our own lists, using the themes below!

191. Creative ways aliens can take over the Earth.

192. Special abilities humans can have.

193. Animals that can mutate into super-beasts.

194. Mythological characters who can be worked into a modern work.

195. Planets in your fictional universe.

196. Power words you want to work into your story.

197. Character traits for your hero, villain, and sidekick.

198. Timeline events.

199. Similes and metaphors for your world.

200. Nouns that remind you of darkness, victory, or hope.

201. Numbers that have meaning to you (or your story) and why.

202. Sounds that you (or your character) hear.

203. Things that inspire you about the night sky, the forest, or the desert.

204. Magical properties and how they work.

205. Unbreakable promises.

206. Onomatopoeia-types of sounds. (Boom, crash, twack, etc.)

207. Character flaws.

208. Symbols that have meaning.

209. Foods in your fictional world.

Prompt # _____ Your Title: _____

Prompt # _____ Your Title: _____

Prompt # _____ Your Title: _____

LUNE

A Practice in Brevity

Writing Challenge:

Diversify your topics and include lunes: about a friend, a family member, and something romantic. Then tap into some emotions: happiness, sadness, indifference, or need.

What is a lune, you ask? A lune is a short poem similar to a haiku. The lune has a syllable pattern of 5/3/5. (Whereas, the popular haiku follows a 5/7/5 syllable pattern.)

Here are some samples:

Something a little silly:

A shriek of sadness 5
Tumbling, 3
I dropped my ice cream. 5

—Robin Woods

They can be romantic:

Warmth like liquid fire. 5
Your heart song 3
Sets my soul ablaze. 5

—Robin Woods

Or even sinister:

Darkness swirled inside, 5
Itching to 3
Come out and destroy. 5

—Robin Woods

Now, it's your turn to write a lune.

210. Write a lune about nature:

_____

_____

_____

211. About love:

_____

_____

_____

212. About loss:

_____

_____

_____

213. About joy:

_____

_____

_____

214. About friendship:

_____

_____

_____

215. About a myth:

_____

_____

_____

JOURNAL

REFERENCE

Legendary Creatures

Antelopes	Gilled Antelope (Cambodian) deer who breathes water Goldhorn (Slavic) golden horned white antelope
Aquatic Beings	Bake-kujira (Japanese) a ghost whale Encantado (Brazilian) shape-shifting trickster dolphins Kelpie (Scottish) water horse Selkie (Scottish) shape-shifting seal people
Arthropods	Anansi (West African) trickster spider Arachne (Greek) weaver cursed into a spider Khepri (Ancient Egyptian) beetle who pushes the sun Mothman (American) large humanoid figure with wings and glowing red eyes Scorpion Man (Babylonian) protector of travelers Selket (Egyptian) scorpion death and healing goddess
Bats	Camazotz (Mayan) death bat or bat-god Vampire (Worldwide) undead human, often a shape-shifter
Bears	Bugbear (Celtic) child-eating sprite Callisto (Greek) nymph turned into a bear by Hera Nandi Bear (African) large, ferocious bear with a sloping back like a hyena Nanook (Inuit) master of bears who decides if hunters deserve success
Birds	Cetan (Native American) hawk spirit Chamrosh (Persian myth) body of a dog, head & wings of a bird Chol (Biblical mythology) phoenix Griffin (Greek) king of all creatures, part lion & part eagle who guards treasure Harpy (Greek) half-human & half-bird women who steal food and evil people
Canine	Black dog (British) Hellhound Cerberus (Greek & Roman) multi-headed dog at Gate of the Underworld Chupacabra (Puerto Rican & South American) blood-drinking creature of the night Hellhound (Worldwide) supernatural dog, bringers of death
Equines	Centaur (Greek) torso and up human, the body and legs down horse Cheval Gauvin (French & Swiss) a rider-killing horse Haizum (Islam) horse of the archangel Gabriel Hippocamp (Greek) sea horse Pegasus (Greek) white-winged horse Pooka (Irish) spirits or fairies who lived near ancient stones Uchchaihshravas (Hindu) seven-headed, all white flying horse Unicorn (Worldwide) horse with a single horn

Feline	Beast of Bodmin Moor (British) phantom wildcat Chimera (Greek) hybrid lion with a second goat head and snake tail Manticore (Persian) human head, body of a lion, and scorpion's tail Sphinix (Egyptian) guardian with the head of a human, body of a lion Werecat (Worldwide) people who transform into cats
Fish	Abaia (Melanesian) gigantic, freshwater, lake-dwelling eel who protects the lake Merperson (Worldwide) half-human, half-fish Namanzu (Japanese) giant catfish responsible for earthquakes Water Spirit (Worldwide) supernatural spirit
Mollusks	Kraken (Worldwide) squid monster Shen (Chinese) clam monster
Pachyderm	Baku (Japanese) supernatural beings that devour dreams and nightmares Ganesh (Hindu) elephant-headed deity who is the remover of obstacles
Primates	Bigfoot or Sasquatch (North America) Cryptid, animal of the Northwest Jué yuán (Japanese) blue-furred, man-sized, rhesus monkey that abducts women Satori (Japanese) mind-reading magical primate Yeti or Abominable Snowman (Nepalese) large, mysterious ape-like entity
Rabbits & Hares	Al-mi'raj (Arabian) rabbit with unicorn horn Jackalope (North American) fearsome jackrabbit with antelope horns Moon Rabbit (Aztec & Chinese) rabbit who lives on the moon
Reptiles, Serpents & worms	Amphisbaena (Mediterranean) ant-eating serpent with a head at each end Amphithere (European) winged serpent Apophis (Egyptian) Lord of Chaos Bakonawa (Filipino) giant serpent who is the cause of eclipses Basilisk (European) king of serpents, kills with a single glance Cipactli (Spanish) sea monster with a thousand mouths, part crocodile, fish, & toad Cockatrice (British) two-legged dragon with a rooster head Drake (European) large, fire breathing dragon Echidna (Greek) half-human, half-snake she-viper who was the mother of monsters Gorgon (Greek) sisters with hair of living snakes who can turn people to stone Hydra (Greek & Roman) many headed water monster with regenerative heads Jaculus (Greek) tree-dwelling dragon associated with the javelin Mongolian Death Worm (Mongolian) desert-dwelling, venom-spitting, electrical worm Naga (Worldwide) dragon or snake associated with nature Ouroboros (Egyptian & Greek) serpent who eats its own tail Tarasque (French) dragon with a lion's head Wyvern (European & British) two-legged dragon

Non-Human Character Appearance Charts

Eye Color	Amber	Cerulean Blue	Electric Blue	Cobalt	Coal
	Glowing	Star Fire	Liquid Metal	Gold	Pewter
	Burgundy	Gold	Obsidian	Silver	Slate
	Lava	Sage	Aqua	Amethyst	Fuchsia
	Buttercream	Terracotta	Scarlet	Copper	White
	Spanish Moss	Other:			
Eye Descriptors	Angular	Bulbous	Cat-like	Circular	Hooded
	Concave	Cone-like	Lidless	Protruding	Slashes
	Deep-set	Other:			
Skin	Iridescent	Scaly	Slimy	Crusted	Patchy
	Translucent	Mottled	Stripped	Spotted	Potholed
	Freckled	Oozing	Festering	Fissured	Pustule
	Ulcerative	Papery	Uneven	Glass-like	Pore-less
	Other:				
Body Descriptors	Spindly	Amorphous	Anthropomorphic	Exoskeleton	Rigid
	Octopoid	Insectoid	Non-Vertebrate	Mechanical	Xenophobe
	Other:				
Facial Shapes	Circular	Bulbous	Spade-like	Diamond	Cone
	Block	Jowly	Pickaxe	Elongated	Spiraled
	Other:				
Hair Descriptors	Straw	Silk	Rubber	Feathered	Sea Grass
	Tinsel	Gelatinous	Rope-like	Spinney	Spikes
	Coarse Fur	Coral	Sharp	Slithering	Mossy
	Other:				

Notes:

Human Character Appearance Charts

Eye Color	Blue	Sky Blue	Baby Blue	Electric Blue	Cornflower
	Brown	Chestnut	Chocolate	Cognac	Amber
	Green	Sea Green	Moss Green	Jade	Emerald
	Grey	Silver	Gunmetal Grey	Charcoal	Black
	Hazel	Russet	Nut	Honey	Yellow
	Lavender	Other:			
Eye Shape	Almond	Round	Drooping	Hooded	Close-set
	Wide-set	Deep-set	Protruding	Sleepy	Squinting
	Down-turned	Other:			
Skin Tone	Fair	Ivory	Porcelain	Milk	Snow
	Ruddy	Rose	Peach	Ochre	Golden
	Olive	Khaki	Toffee	Honey	Tawny
	Dark	Ebony	Sepia	Russet	Mahogany
	Other:				
Body Shape	Triangle	Rectangle	Hourglass	Rounded	Diamond
	Inverted Triangle	Barrel	Willowy	Husky	Wiry
	Other:				
Facial Shapes	Oval	Rectangle	Square	Heart	Oblong
	Egg	Diamond	Triangle	Narrow	Block-like
	Other:				
Hair Color	Black	Dark Brown	Medium Brown	Ash Brown	Golden Brown
	Red	Auburn	Copper	Strawberry	Cinnamon
	Blond	Platinum	White	Silver	Grey
	Other:				

Notes:

Character Traits

All characters, even good ones, should have some reasonable flaws. And in turn, characters that are purely evil often appear fake. It is best to have a healthy mix of believable traits. Here is a list to get you thinking:

Positive Traits				
Adaptable	Accepting	Adventurous	Affectionate	Amiable
Alert	Astute	Benevolent	Brave	Charismatic
Creative	Decisive	Dependable	Diplomatic	Disciplined
Earnest	Efficient	Empathetic	Enthusiastic	Ethical
Fair	Forgiving	Good-hearted	Gracious	Happy
Hard-working	Independent	Insightful	Intelligent	Just
Leader	Loving	Nurturing	Orderly	Patient
Passionate	Persuasive	Playful	Responsible	Resourceful
Self-aware	Spunky	Strong	Studious	Supportive
Tactful	Tenacious	Unselfish	Watchful	Wise

Negative Traits				
Abusive	Addictive	Aggressive	Antisocial	Apathetic
Argumentative	Belligerent	Callous	Cantankerous	Childish
Clingy	Closed-minded	Cocky	Compulsive	Cowardly
Cruel	Cynical	Dangerous	Deceitful	Defensive
Degrading	Destructive	Disloyal	Egocentric	Evil
Fearful	Fixated	Flaky	Foolish	Forgetful
Hostile	Hung-up	Insecure	Loner	Megalomaniacal
Neurotic	Phobic	Perfectionist	Pessimistic	Prejudiced
Manipulative	Selfish	Self-destructive	Stubborn	Sulker
Touchy	Unreceptive	Vengeful	Whiney	Withdrawn

Number Symbolism

Choosing numbers that have symbolic meaning and weight can add depth to your narrative. We see it in literature all the time—three little pigs, seven dwarves, etc.

Popular Symbolic Numbers	
Two	Duality, partnership, male & female, yin & yang, left & right, hot & cold, sun & moon, night & day, active & passive, other:
Three	Trinity (Father, Son, & Holy Spirit), circle of life (birth, life, & death), idea of self (mind, body, & spirit), mystical number in folktales (three wishes, three challenges, three guesses, etc.), three rulers in Greek mythology (Zeus, Hades, & Poseidon), three Fates, Shakespeare's *Macbeth* has three witches, other:
Four	Four elements (earth, air, wind, & fire), four cardinal points (north, south, east, & west), humanity (four limbs), four seasons, four humors (blood, choler, phlegm, & black bile), four phases of the moon, four horseman of the Apocalypse, other:
Six	Satan, evil, the devil, other:
Seven	Trinity plus humanity (3+4), days of the week, seven deadly sins, other:
Nine	Nine lives of a cat, Norse mythology there are nine worlds, Greek mythology there are nine Muses, other:
Twelve	A complete cycle, twelve months, twelve hours, twelve disciples of Christ, twelve tribes of Israel, twelve inches in a foot, other:
Thirteen	Unlucky, bad luck, Judas was the thirteenth person to arrive to the last supper, other:
Forty	Trials and tribulations, Hebrews wandered for forty years, other:
Notes:	

Tastes and Aromas

When you are writing, try to incorporate all four of the senses in your work. Here is a cheat sheet for tastes and smells:

Positive	Neutral	Negative	Spices	Florals (Most Fragrant)
Aromatic	Acidic	Biting	Cajun	Angel's Trumpet
Citrusy	Acrid	Bitter	Cinnamon	Flowering Plum
Comforting	Airy	Decay	Clove	Heliotrope
Crisp	Ancient	Dirty	Coriander	Honeysuckle
Delicate	Brackish	Fetid	Cumin	Jasmine
Delicious	Burnt	Foul	Dill	Lavender
Exquisite	Delicate	Funky	Pepper	Lilac
Fragrant	Feminine	Gamy	Sage	Mexican Orange
Fresh	Fermented	Harsh	Thyme	Mock Orange
Fruity	Masculine	Moldy	Basil	Rose
Full-bodied	Floral	Musty	Barbeque	Star Magnolia
Hard	Humid	Nasty	Bay Leaf	Sweet Peas
Heady	Light	Noxious	Curry	Tuberose
Juicy	Medicinal	Old	Anise	
Lemony	Medium	Pungent	Caraway Seed	**Household Smells**
Rich	Mellow	Putrid	Cardamom	Babies
Savory	Metallic	Rancid	Cayenne	"Boy" Smell
Sharp	Mild	Rank	Cumin	Bacon
Succulent	Minty	Repulsive	Dill	BBQ
Sugary	Moist	Rotting	Fennel	Beer
Sweet	Musky	Skunky	Garlic	Books
Tangy	Nippy	Sour	Ginger	Bread
Tart	Nutty	Spoiled	Mace	Burning Wood
Tempting	Peppery	Stagnant	Marjoram	Chocolate
Warm	Perfumed	Stale	Mint	Cinnamon
Woody	Salty	Stench	Mustard	Citrus
Zesty	Woodsy	Stinking	Onion	Coconut
Zingy	Yeasty	Stuffy	Orange Peel	Coffee
			Lemon Peel	Cut Grass
Other:	Other:	Other:	Nutmeg	Dirty Laundry
			Rosemary	Fresh-baked Cookies
			Saffron	Fresh Laundry
			Turmeric	Pine
			Vanilla	Soap

Synonyms

As you are editing, it is important to pay attention to repetition. Much of the tinkering with words will come with editing, but I love using synonym sheets to cut down on the editing later, as well as to inspire me.

Emotions

Other words for Happy

Alluring, amused, appealing, appeased, blissful, blithe, carefree, charmed, cheeky, chipper, chirpy, content, convivial, delighted, elated, electrified, ecstatic, enchanted, enthusiastic, exultant, excited, fantastic, fulfilled, glad, gleeful, glowing, gratified, idyllic, intoxicating, jolly, joyful, joyous, jovial, jubilant, light, lively, merry, mirthful, overjoyed, pleased, pleasant, radiant, sparkling, savoured, satisfied, serene, sunny, thrilled, tickled, up, upbeat, winsome, wonderful.

Other words for SAD

Aching, agitated, anguished, anxious, bleak, bothered, brooding, bugged, chagrined, cheerless, darkly, disillusioned, disappointed, disenchanted, disheartened, dismayed, distraught, dissatisfied, despondent, doleful, failed, faint, frustrated, glazed, gloomy, glowering, haunted, hopeless, languid, miserable, pained, perturbed, sour, suffering, sullen, thwarted, tormented, troubled, uneasy, unsettled, upset, vacant, vexed, wan, woeful, wounded.

Other words for Mad

Affronted, aggravated, agitated, angered, annoyed, bitter, boiling, bothered, brooding, bugged, bummed, cantankerous, chafed, chagrined, crabby, cross, disgruntled, distraught, disturbed, enflamed, enraged, exasperated, fiery, fuming, furious, frantic, galled, goaded, hacked, heated, hostile, hot, huffy, ill-tempered, incensed, indignant, inflamed, infuriated, irate, ireful, irritated, livid, maddened, malcontent, miffed, nettled, offended, peeved, piqued, provoked, raging, resentful, riled, scowling, sore, sour, stung, taut, tense, tight, troubled, upset, vexed, wrathful.

Other words for Crying

Bawling, blubbering, gushing, howling, lamenting, moaning, scream-crying, silent tears, sniffling, snivelling, sobbing, sorrowing, teary, wailing, weepy, woeful.

Commonly Used Words

Other words for ASKED

Appealed, begged, beckoned, beseeched, besieged, bid, craved, commanded, claimed, coaxed, challenged, charged, charmed, cross-examined, demanded, drilled, entreated, enchanted, grilled, implored, imposed, interrogated, invited, invoked, inquired, insisted, needled, ordered, pleaded, petitioned, picked, probed, pried, pressed, pumped, pursued, put through the wringer, put the screws down, questioned, queried, quizzed, requested, required, requisitioned, roasted, solicited, summoned, surveyed, sweated, urged, wanted, wheedled, wooed, worried, wondered.

Other words for LAUGH

Break up, burst, cackle, chortle, chuckle, crack-up, crow, giggle, grin, guffaw, hee-haw, howl, peal, quack, roar, scream, shriek, snicker, snigger, snort, split one's sides, tee-hee, titter, whoop.

Other Words for LOOK

Address, admire, attention, audit, babysit, beam, beholding, blink, bore, browse, burn, cast, check, comb, consider, contemplate, delve, detect, discover, disregard, distinguish, ensure, evil eye, examine, explore, eye, eyeball, ferret, fix, flash, forage, gander, gaze, get an eyeful, give the eye, glance, glare, glaze, glimmer, glimpse, glitter, gloat, goggle, grope, gun, have a gander, inquire, inspect, investigate, judge, keeping watch, leaf-through, leer, lock daggers on, look fixedly, look-see, marking, moon, mope, neglect, note, notice, noting, observe, ogle, once-over, peek, peep, peer, peg, peruse, poke into, scan, pout, probe, pry, quest, rake, recognize, reconnaissance, regard, regarding, renew, resemble, review, riffle, rubberneck, rummage, scan, scowl, scrutinize, search, seeing, sense, settle, shine, sift, simper, size-up, skim, slant, smile, smirk, snatch, sneer, speculative, spot, spy, squint, stare, study, sulk, supervise, surveillance, survey, sweep, take stock of, take in, trace, verify, view, viewing, watch, witness, yawp, zero in.

Other words for REPLIED

Acknowledged, answered, argued, accounted, barked, bit, be in touch, boomeranged, comeback, countered, conferred, claimed, denied, echoed, feedback, fielded the question, get back to, growled, matched, parried, reacted, reciprocated, rejoined, responded, retorted, remarked, returned, retaliated, shot back, snapped, squelched, squared, swung, vacillated.

Other words for Sat

Be seated, bear on, cover, ensconce, give feet a rest, grab a chair, have a place, have a seat, hunker, install, lie, park, perch, plop down, pose, posture, put it there, relax, remain, rest, seat, seat oneself, settle, squat, take a load off, take a place, take a seat.

Other words for Was/Were   VERB (TO BE)

Abided, acted, be alive, befell, breathed, continued, coexisted, do, endured, ensued, existed, had been, happened, inhabited, lasted, lived, moved, obtained, occurred, persisted, prevailed, remained, rested, stood, stayed, survived, subsided, subsisted, transpired.

Other words for Walk

Advance, amble, barge, bolt, bounce, bound, canter, charge, crawl, creep, dance, dash, escort, gallop, hike, hobble, hop, jog, jump, leap, limp, lope, lumber, meander, mosey, move, pad, pace march, parade, patrol, plod, prance, proceed, promenade, prowl, race, roam, rove, run, sashay, saunter, scamper, scramble, zip shuffle, skip, slink, slither, slog, sprint, stagger, step, stomp, stride, stroll, strut, stumble, swagger, thread, tiptoe, traipse, tramp, tread, trek, trip, trot, trudge, wade, wander.

Other words for Whisper

Breathed, buzz, disclosed, exhaled, expressed, fluttered, gasped, hint, hiss, hum, hushed tone, intoned, lament, low voice, moaned, mouthed, mumble, murmur, mutter, puff, purred, rasped, reflected, ruffle, rumble, rush, said low, said softly, sigh, sob, undertone, utter, voiced, wheezed.

Other words for Went

Abscond, ambled, approached, avoided, be off, beat it, bolted, bounced, bounded, bugged out, burst, carved, cleared out, crawled, crept, cruised, cut and run, danced, darted, dashed, decamped, deserted, disappeared, ducked out, escaped, evaded, exited, fared, fled, floated, flew, flew the coop, galloped, got away, got going, got lost, glided, go down, go south, hightailed, hit the road, hoofed it, hopped, hotfooted, hurdled, hustled, journeyed, jumped, leapt, left, lighted out, loped, lunged, made haste, made a break for it, made for, made off, made tracks, marched, moseyed, moved, muscled, neared, negotiated, paced, paraded, passed, pedaled, proceeded, progressed, pulled out, pulled, pushed off, pushed on, quitted, retired, retreated, rode, ran along, ran away, rushed, sashayed, scampered, scooted, scrammed, scurried, scuttled, set off, set out, shot, shouldered, shoved off, shuffled, skedaddled, skipped out, skipped, skirted, slinked, slipped, soared, split, sprang, sprinted, stole away, steered clear, stepped on it, strolled, strutted, scurried, swept, took a hike, took a powder, took flight, took leave, took off, threaded, toddled, tottered, trampled, travelled, traversed, trekked, trode, trudged, tumbled, vamoosed, vanished, vaulted, veered, walked off, wandered, weaved, wended, whisked, withdrew, wormed, zipped, zoomed.

Other words for **SAID**

accused, acknowledged, added, announced, addressed, admitted, advised, affirmed, agreed, asked, avowed, asserted, answered, apologized, argued, assured, approved, articulated, alleged, attested, barked, bet, bellowed, babbled, begged, bragged, began, bawled, bleated, blurted, boomed, broke in, bugged, boasted, bubbled, beamed, burst out, believed, brought out, confided, crowed, coughed, cried, congratulated, complained, conceded, chorused, concluded, confessed, chatted, convinced, chattered, cheered, chided, chimed in, clucked, coaxed, commanded, cautioned, continued, commented, called, croaked, chuckled, claimed, choked, chortled, corrected, communicated, claimed, contended, criticized, construe,

dared, decided, disagreed, described, disclosed, drawled, denied, declared, demanded, divulged, doubted, denied, disputed, dictated, echoed, ended, exclaimed, explained, expressed, enunciated, expounded, emphasized, formulated, fretted, finished, gulped, gurgled, gasped, grumbled, groaned, guessed, gibed, giggled, greeted, growled, grunted, hinted, hissed, hollered, hypothesized, inquired, imitated, implied, insisted, interjected, interrupted, intoned, informed, interpreted, illustrated, insinuated, jeered, jested, joked, justified, lied, laughed, lisped, maintained, muttered, marveled, moaned, mimicked, mumble, modulated, murmured, mused, mentioned, mouthed, nagged, noted, nodded, noticed,

objected, observed, offered, ordered, owned up, piped, pointed out, panted, pondered, praised, prayed, puzzled, proclaimed, promised, proposed, protested, purred, pled, pleaded, put in, prevailed, parried, pressed, put forward, pronounced, pointed out, prescribed, popped off, persisted, protested, questioned, quavered, quipped, quoted, queried, rejected, reasoned, ranted, rasped, reassured, reminded, responded, recalled, returned, requested, roared, related, remarked, replied, reported, revealed, rebutted, retorted, repeated, reckoned, remembered, regarded, recited, resolved, reflected, ripped, rectified, reaffirmed,

snickered, sniffed, smirked, snapped, snarled, shot, sneered, sneezed, started, stated, stormed, sobbed, stuttered, suggested, surmised, sassed, sputtered, sniffled, snorted, spoke, stammered, squeaked, sassed, scoffed, scolded, screamed, shouted, sighed, smiled, sang, shrieked, shrilled, speculated, supposed, settled, solved, shot back, swore, stressed, spilled, told, tested, trilled, taunted, teased, tempted, theorized, threatened, tore, uttered, unveiled, urged, upheld, vocalized, voiced, vindicated, volunteered, vowed, vented, verbalized, warned, wailed, went on, wept, whimpered, whined, wondered, whispered, worried, warranted, yawned, yakked.

My Lists:

Other Notes & Research

Bibliography for the Legendary Creatures

Cotterell, Arthur and Rachel Storm. *The Ultimate Anthology of Mythology*. Hermes House, 1999.

Guiley, Rosemary Ellen. *The Encyclopedia of Angels*. 2nd Edition. Checkmark Books: USA, 2004.

Guiley, Rosemary Ellen. *Vampires, Werewolves, & Other Monsters. Checkmark Books*, USA. 2005.

Montague, Charlotte. *Monsters and Demons*. New York: Chartwell Books, 2012.

Philip, Neil. *The Illustrated Book of Myths: Tales & Legends of the World*. New York: DK Publishing, 1995.

Other Referenced Material

Bradbury, Ray. *Zen in the Art of Writing: Essays on Creativity*. Santa Barbara: Joshua Odell Editions, 1996.

"Highlights from the Mechanical Curator: Highlights from more than one million public domain images." from The British Library. https://www.flickr.com/photos/britishlibrary/sets/72157638544764936/page1/

King, Stephen. *On Writing: A Memoir of the Craft*. Anniversary edition. New York: Scribner, 2010.

Books by Robin Woods

Young Adult Fiction

Allure: A Watcher Series Prequel

The Unintended: The Watcher Series Book One

The Nexus: The Watcher Series Book Two

The Sacrifice: The Watcher Series Book Three

The Fallen: Part One: Watcher Series Book Four

The Fallen: Part Two: Watcher Series Book Five

  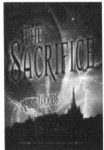   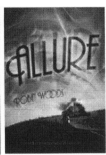

Non-Fiction

Prompt Me Workbook & Journal

Prompt Me Again Workbook & Journal

Prompt Me More Workbook & Journal

Prompt Me Sci-Fi & Fantasy Workbook & Journal

Prompt Me Romance Workbook & Journal

Prompt Me Novel Formerly
Fiction Writing Workbook & Journal

More Prompt Me Series in 2019 **Prompt Me Kids, Prompt Me Classroom,** and more.

Robin Woods is a former high school and university instructor with two and a half decades of experience teaching English, literature, and writing. She earned a BA in English and an MA in education.

In addition to teaching, she has published six highly rated novels and has multiple projects in the works, including writing for a Hollywood producer.

When Ms. Woods isn't chasing her two elementary school kids around, she's spending time with her ever-patient husband.

For more information and free resources, go to her website at:

www.RobinWoodsFiction.com

Made in the
USA
Columbia, SC